BODIES IN
CRISIS

DRUGS AND
DISEASE

Jacqueline L. Harris

TFCB

Twenty-First Century Books

A Division of Henry Holt and Company
New York

Twenty-First Century Books
A Division of Henry Holt and Company, Inc.
115 West 18th Street
New York, New York 10011

Henry Holt® and colophon are registered trademarks of Henry Holt and
Company, Inc.
Publishers since 1866

Published in Canada by Fitzhenry & Whiteside Ltd.
195 Allstate Parkway, Markham, Ontario L3R 4T8

Printed in Mexico
All first editions are printed on acid-free paper.

Created and produced in association with Blackbirch Graphics, Inc.

Library of Congress Cataloging-in-Publication Data

Harris, Jacqueline L.
    Drugs and disease / Jacqueline L. Harris. — 1st. ed.
        p.   cm. — (Bodies in crisis)
    Includes bibliographical references and index.
    Summary: Explains the nature of drugs, their effects on the body, the patterns and
biological causes of addiction, and the consequences of drug abuse.
    ISBN 0-8050-2602-9 (acid-free paper)
    1. Drug abuse—Juvenile literature. 2. Psychotropic drugs—Juvenile literature.
[1. Drugs. 2. Drug abuse.] I. Title. II. Series.
    RC564.3.H37 1993
    616.86—dc20   93-25912
                                                                          CIP
                                                                           AC

Contents

Many common drugs change the way the human body works. If abused, most of these substances can cause severe, long-term damage.

Dangers of Abuse

A healthy human body works by coordinating thousands of internal and external functions. Each minute you are alive, your body is performing many tiny chemical reactions, some of which help you to breathe, digest, fight infection, circulate blood, and generate new cells as old ones die. Properly fed and rested, the human body can go on functioning for years.

Sometimes various factors can disrupt the healthy functioning of the body. These factors, among many, may be hereditary (passed on by parents), they may be environmental (caused by elements in the surroundings), or they may be brought on by particular personal behaviors, such as poor diet, smoking, or insufficient sleep. One other type of personal behavior that can cause mental and physical diseases is the overuse, or abuse, of drugs.

Different Drugs for Different Purposes

A drug is a chemical that changes the way a part of the body works. Most legal drugs are designed to be taken in limited quantities and for very specific periods of time. Some drugs are designed to help the body recover from illness, avoid disease, or battle certain emotional problems. Other drugs are found in substances people consume every day: caffeine is in coffee, tea, cola, aspirin, and chocolate; nicotine is in cigarettes; alcohol is in beer, wine, liquor, and many food flavorings. Still other drugs—many of them illegal—do not serve any medical, therapeutic, or food-related purpose. These drugs are consumed simply for the effects they create on the mind and body. Any kind of drug, however— legal or illegal—can be abused.

In fact, abuse of almost any substance can cause health problems. Even substances that are as seemingly harmless as coffee, cough medicine, aspirin, or laxatives can seriously affect the body if these substances are abused. For the most part, drug-related diseases

Most households contain legal drugs that are designed to help sick people feel better. But even these common drugs can become dangerous if they are abused.

occur as a result of constant and excessive use; in the majority of cases, the abuser has become physically dependent on a drug and must continue to take increasing amounts of it in order to function or to feel good. This physical dependency occurs when a drug is taken so frequently that the body of the user begins to rely on the drug in order to function. As the body relies more and more on the drug, the abuser becomes more and more dependent on the drug to function.

How Drugs Work

Drugs act on the body by producing special chemical reactions or by changing normal chemical reactions. These reactions affect the functioning of many parts of the body. Some drugs stop pain. Others change the way the heart works. Still others speed up or slow down the action of the intestinal walls or make the body produce more urine. Drugs can lower blood pressure, kill disease organisms, and spur organs to produce powerful chemicals called hormones.

Drugs can also affect the mind—making people feel calm, happy, or nervous or causing them to see things that aren't there (hallucinate). Drugs can put people to sleep, make them agitated or violent, or help them to remember or to forget.

Doctors use drugs to help sick people. During their medical education, doctors learn what drugs are, how they work, and how they affect people. This training enables doctors to decide on what kind and what amount of a drug will best help a patient with a specific illness. But drug abusers do not use drugs because they need them medically. Instead, they use them for the pleasure they provide, and they don't understand or care that drugs, when used improperly, can do a great deal of harm to their bodies.

Some Reasons for Drug Abuse

Why do people abuse drugs? There are a number of reasons. Some people are simply curious; they want to see what drugs will do to their bodies, and so they start experimenting with them. This experimentation often leads to dependency. Other people use drugs because their friends are using them. If they are with a group of peers, they may want to join in with everyone else— especially if their friends say, "Come on. Try it."

Peer pressure is often one of the most powerful influences on teens who try to avoid using drugs.

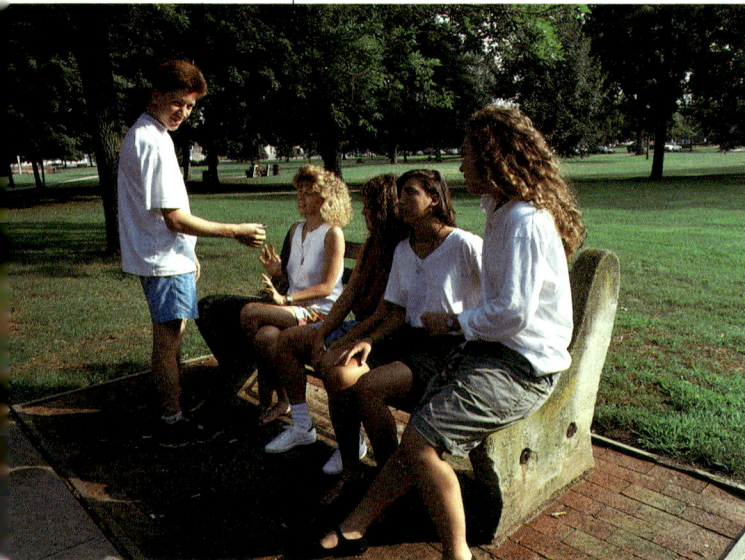

People sometimes rely on drugs to perform better in stressful situations. Stimulants, for example, may be taken by students facing exams, motorists driving long distances, soldiers going into battle, or athletes about to enter competition. Other people abuse drugs because they have a low opinion of themselves or because they have problems in their lives. Drugs can make these people feel better and, for a short time, allow them to forget their troubles.

Illegal drugs that affect the brain are the ones most often taken by drug abusers. These drugs are also called psychoactive, or mind-altering, drugs. The brain controls the body and mind through a complex system of nerve cells. These nerve cells send and receive signals, while chemicals in the brain make it possible for the signals to be transmitted. When a person takes a psychoactive drug, the drug changes the brain's normal signal network. A person with altered signals in the brain often gets a "high," or good feeling.

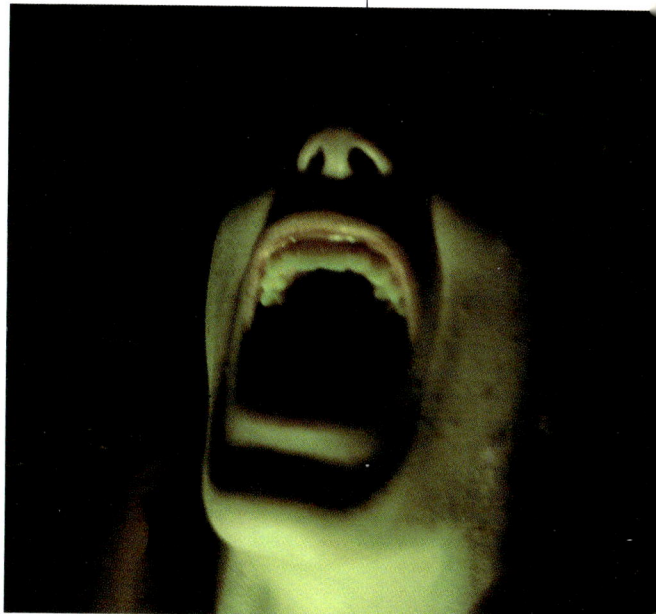

Withdrawal can be one of the most painful consequences of drug addiction.

The Dangers of Drugs

A drug abuser runs many risks. Perhaps the worst risk is that of becoming an addict—of giving one's life over to the need for a chemical. A person who uses a drug just once is not considered an addict. A drug abuser uses a drug regularly, and this causes the brain to adjust to the chemical. This adjustment is referred to as physical drug dependence, or addiction. If the addicted person fails to take the drug, the brain tries to adjust to the lack of the drug. The brain then sends out signals that cause the person to suffer the consequences of not having the drug. This is called withdrawal. Withdrawal may cause vomiting, sweating, trembling, and convulsions (fainting, twitching, and jerking of the arms and legs).

Some abusers become only psychologically drug-dependent. That means they crave the good feelings produced by a drug. When they do not take the drug, withdrawal is milder, but it produces anger, moodiness, impatience, and nervousness.

Constant use of most drugs can damage both the body and the mind. Alcohol and many other drugs can damage the liver, the body's main chemical factory. Marijuana and tobacco damage the lungs and can produce breathing problems. Abuse of caffeine and nicotine can cause heart problems as well as possible problems with the bladder. Some drugs used by pregnant women—even in small doses—can damage their unborn babies.

Drug addiction can also cause harm in less direct ways. Many addicts lose their appetites and forget to eat. Poor nutrition lowers their resistance to infection, which exposes them to lung diseases such as tuberculosis and pneumonia. Abusers also run the risk of developing bleeding in the brain (stroke) and tremors (shaking). Because continuous drug use can kill brain cells, drug abusers may begin having problems with their memory, thought processes, and speech.

Teens at Risk

Teenagers who abuse drugs to ease the problems of everyday life run the risk of ruining their lives forever. Teen drug abusers ruin their chances for a good education and never really learn to cope with the ups and downs of life. When these teens get older—even if they

America's Drug Use at a Glance

- The 1992 National Household Survey on Drug Abuse found that 6.2% of Americans age 12 and older were drug users.
- Illegal drug use among youths 12 to 17 years old declined in 1991 from 14.9% to 6.8%.
- Marijuana is the most commonly used illegal drug in America. Cocaine ranks second.
- The most commonly abused legal drug in America is alcohol.
- A National Health Survey in 1988 found that more than 15 million people in the United States exhibited symptoms of alcohol abuse, alcohol dependence, or both.
- About 25% of the American population smokes cigarettes.

eventually quit abusing drugs—they may have trouble fitting into the adult world. With few options and poor skills, many of these people also go on to create serious problems for the rest of society. Most often, they wind up in mental institutions or prisons, and many die from overdoses.

Drug abuse affects society in other ways, too. A number of auto accidents are caused by people under the influence of drugs. Addicts and drug abusers are among the most likely individuals to attack other people, either for money or simply because they have gone out of control. Those who need money to buy drugs will often burglarize homes, steal automobiles, and rob and terrorize people to get a "fix" of the drug they crave.

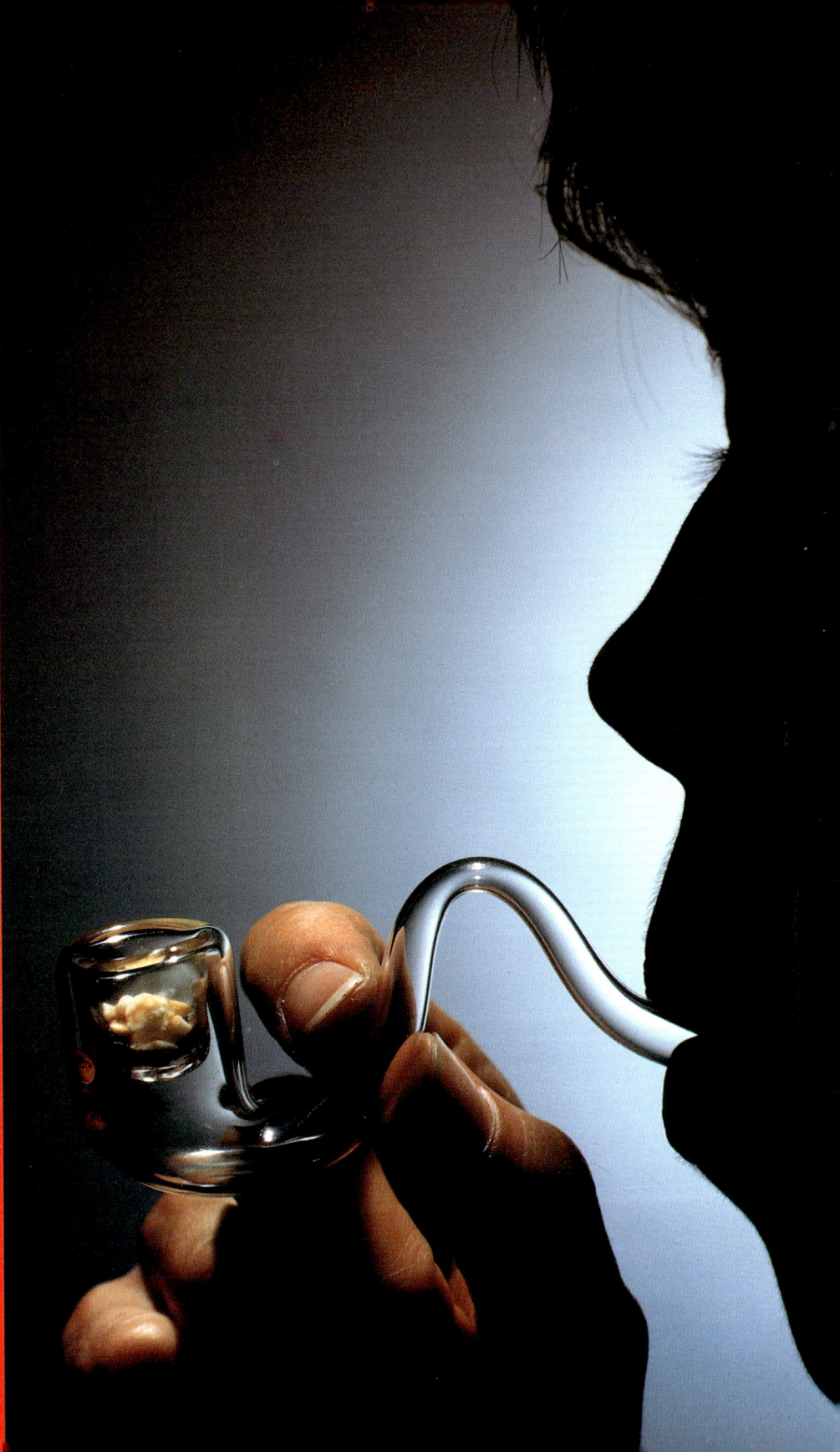

A young girl smokes crack, one of the most powerful and dangerous stimulants. Because of its concentration, crack provides an almost instant effect and a strong psychological dependence.

Stimulants and Psychedelics: Speeding Up the Action of the Brain

Jack felt tired and sad, so he popped two black capsules into his mouth. Within minutes, the drug began to work. The tiredness and sadness he had felt turned to a wide-awake and happy feeling. But later Jack began to imagine that bugs were crawling under the skin of his arm. He dug at his arm, scratching and rubbing, trying to kill the bugs. Soon he had produced several bleeding sores on his arm, but still he could not seem to kill the imaginary bugs. He had abused a stimulant—a drug that is a powerful brain activator.

There are two kinds of brain activators—stimulants and psychedelics.

Stimulants act on the brain to increase breathing, heart-beat, and blood pressure. People who take these drugs often feel energetic and very happy; they are stimulated. But sometimes they become too stimulated, and their heart races, their blood pressure goes up, they become nervous and worry a lot, and they can't seem to keep their mind on anything. Drugs that are stimulants include amphetamines, cocaine-crack, nicotine, and caffeine.

Amphetamines

Amphetamines, which are manufactured by drug companies, were at one time commonly prescribed by doctors to treat certain illnesses. There are approximately 50 kinds of amphetamines. In the past, amphetamines that lessen the appetite were given to people to help them lose weight. Others cleared stuffy noses. However, amphetamines were found to be very addictive and are now seldom prescribed by doctors.

Drug abusers use a number of slang, or street, names to describe amphetamines. They include *speed, uppers, bennies, dexies, black beauties, hearts, meth, pep pills, peaches, and lid poppers.*

How Amphetamines Work

Amphetamines block nerve signals coming from the brain that tell the body it is hungry or tired. The result is that the body uses up its stored energy—energy that could be needed in an emergency to fuel important life processes such as breathing and heartbeat. This causes abusers to feel energetic and elated, but at the same time, their bodies cease to function properly.

Harmful Effects of Amphetamines

Amphetamines speed up the heartbeat; increase blood pressure; and cause insomnia (sleeplessness), dizziness, headache, and shakiness. They can also make some other conditions worse, such as certain heart and artery diseases and an eye disease called glaucoma. Large amounts of amphetamines can bring on a kind of insanity that causes the abuser to become violent. Since the drug causes the body to use up its energy supplies, abuse can eventually cause the user to drop dead.

A new amphetamine, "ice," was developed by drug dealers in Asia. It is a white powder, also called "speed" or "crank." It is inhaled through the nose or injected into the body. The use of ice can cause severe mental problems as well as damage to the heart and kidneys.

Cocaine

Cocaine is a white powder made from the leaf of the coca plant, which is native to South America, but which is also grown in Africa, Southeast Asia, and Australia. In

A young girl snorts cocaine, a highly addictive stimulant that is also one of the most commonly abused illegal drugs in America.

the late 1800s, cocaine was commonly used by doctors to stop the pain of eye, nose, and throat surgery. It was also an ingredient in other painkillers, cough medicines, and nasal sprays. Cocaine was even used in Coca-Cola. By 1903, a presidential commission found cocaine to be habit-forming, or addictive. It was removed from Coca-Cola and later banned except for medical use. Eventually, other drugs that were nonaddictive replaced cocaine for medical uses.

Drug users call cocaine *snow, Bernice, coke, C, Cecil, girl, lady, flake*, and *happy dust*. They inhale or snort it through the nose or inject it into a vein. It may take minutes for inhaled cocaine powder to reach the brain, but it takes just a few seconds if it is injected. Cocaine triggers certain brain signals, which make people energetic and alert; and other signals, which produce pleasure and a sense of well-being. After a while, the brain gets used to the effects of cocaine. Soon, the brain's signals don't work properly without cocaine, causing addiction.

Abusers take cocaine for the extreme pleasure it produces. Some say they prefer cocaine to eating their favorite foods, being with friends, or having sex. These activities normally stimulate the pleasure center of the brain—but not for cocaine abusers, whose brains rely only on cocaine for pleasure. Some cocaine abusers say that cocaine makes them think better and become stronger. But doctors say that abusers merely imagine they feel that way.

Harmful Effects of Cocaine

Most cocaine abusers notice only the pleasure that the drug provides. But other things are happening to their bodies during drug use. Blood vessels narrow, blood pressure rises, and heartbeat increases. These things can cause a heart attack or a stroke. Constantly sniffing cocaine also injures the lining of the nose by drying out the mucous membranes. Abusers may lose their sense of smell and may have constantly runny noses or even nosebleeds. One role of the liver is to break down chemicals into simpler forms that the body can excrete. But the liver can be permanently damaged by a constant effort to break down cocaine.

Because cocaine affects the workings of the brain, it can also damage the brain. Cocaine users often become nervous, sensitive to noise, anxious, and forgetful. Some become paranoid, believing that everyone wants to harm them, or violent—sometimes they even try to kill themselves or others.

The Most Dangerous Cocaine

Crack, or "rock," a form of cocaine, was developed by drug dealers in the mid-1980s. It looks like small pieces of white gravel, but crack is an extremely strong form of cocaine and one that causes powerful effects. It is one of the most addictive drugs on the street today. It is also cheaper than powdered cocaine and has become the most common form of cocaine used. Crack is heated in a glass pipe and inhaled into the lungs, where it passes into the bloodstream. The cocaine moves through the blood to the brain in just seconds. Since crack is so concentrated, it affects many parts of the body. It disturbs the oil glands in the skin and the muscles of the eyes as well. It makes other muscles in the body twitch, and it also damages the lungs as it passes into the bloodstream on the way to the rest of the body. Both crack and cocaine powder can cause serious damage to the heart, blood vessels, liver, and brain, but the damage from crack is more severe.

Nicotine

Nicotine is found in the tobacco plant. Tobacco leaves are used to make cigarettes, cigars, pipe tobacco, chewing tobacco, and snuff (tobacco that is snorted). When tobacco is smoked in cigarettes, cigars, and pipes, the smoke is drawn into the mouth, throat, and often the lungs. There are three major substances in the smoke that are harmful to the body. One substance is nicotine, an addictive drug. The other two substances, tar and carbon monoxide, are produced by the burning tobacco.

Most nicotine users smoke in order to feel relaxed, which they believe enables them to better cope with stress or to think more clearly. Nicotine is absorbed into

Facts About Tobacco

- Smoking is the single most preventable cause of death in the United States. Each year 400,000 Americans die prematurely as a result of smoking.
- Smoking costs as much as $100 billion a year—for lost productivity, medical bills, insurance premiums, and ventilation expenses and special maintenance in the workplace.
- Smoking is responsible for 30% of all cancer deaths in the United States each year, including 87% of lung-cancer deaths.
- Smoking causes about 30% of heart-disease deaths each year. Among men, smokers are two to three times more likely than nonsmokers to die of heart attacks.
- Each year about 80,000 Americans die from noncancerous chronic lung diseases linked to smoking.
- Pregnant smokers are 10 times more likely to miscarry than nonsmokers.
- Infants born to smokers have a 50% higher risk of developing Sudden Infant Death Syndrome (SIDS) and are 74% more likely to be of low birth weight than are infants born to mothers who do not smoke.
- Nonsmokers exposed to the tobacco smoke of others are at increased risk for various diseases. " Secondhand smoke" kills about 53,000 Americans a year, including 37,000 from heart disease and 4,000 from cancer.

the bloodstream through the skin of the mouth and through the lungs. The blood then carries the nicotine to the brain, where signals go out to many parts of the body. These signals, like those caused by all stimulants, cause heartbeat and blood pressure to increase. In addition, metabolism, the body's use of food for energy, rises, and muscle stimulation increases.

Harmful Effects of Nicotine

While nicotine's effects do not last very long—within 15 to 30 minutes of ingestion, half of the nicotine in the blood is broken down and eliminated in the urine— constant use of nicotine can cause a number of problems. As a result of smoking, people can develop twitching muscles, sensitivity to light, and stomach and intestinal disorders.

Smoking is the single most preventable cause of death in America. Although the number of smokers has steadily decreased in recent years, about 25% of America's adults still smoke.

Moreover, since nicotine is addictive, smokers develop a craving for it, which makes it difficult for them to give up tobacco. They continue to subject their bodies to nicotine's dangers. They also expose themselves to the even more harmful effects of the tars and carbon monoxide that burning tobacco produces.

Other Problems with Tobacco

Tars are particles left over from the burning of tobacco. They coat the sticky air sacs in the lungs and eventually clog them. Clogged air sacs cannot perform their role of providing oxygen to the blood and removing waste gas from the blood. Some air sacs may be destroyed by the tars, causing emphysema, a lung disease. People with emphysema have trouble breathing, and their hearts are damaged by the extra effort required to push blood through the few remaining air sacs in their lungs.

Tars, which cause cancer in laboratory animals, are believed to cause cancers in tobacco users—cancer of the lungs, throat, mouth, and esophagus (the tube that leads from the throat to the stomach).

Carbon monoxide, a gas, is produced when any substance is burned. More gas is produced when there is very little oxygen present—which is the situation inside a cigarette. The carbon monoxide in the smoke that is inhaled into the lungs passes into the bloodstream, where it combines with hemoglobin (protein that makes blood red) in the blood. Hemoglobin is the oxygen carrier in the blood. If some of the hemoglobin is combined with carbon monoxide, however, it cannot

The lungs of a smoker.

carry oxygen. While the body will eventually remove the carbon monoxide, it cannot keep up with a smoker who averages one cigarette every 30 minutes. If carbon monoxide levels increase too much, the body becomes starved for oxygen. This can trigger a heart attack, particularly in a person who suffers from heart disease or is at risk of getting heart disease.

Another condition linked to smoking is the depletion of vitamin C. This vitamin is thought to protect against cancer, make the body more resistant to infection, and prevent changes in body fats that lead to heart disease.

Smoking has also been linked to the development of cataracts, an abnormality of the eye. Pregnant smokers risk having babies with low birth weights and other problems. Smoking also damages the cilia, tiny hairlike structures that sweep disease organisms out of the lungs. A smoker, therefore, is more apt to get colds and lung infections.

Caffeine

Caffeine is a mild stimulant. The drug is produced by the coffee plant, tea plant, and cacao plant (used in making chocolate), the kola-nut plant (used in making certain sodas), and other tropical plants. Parts of these plants are used to make coffee, tea, cocoa, and cola.

How Caffeine Works

Many people drink beverages with caffeine because of the taste, but these drinks are also stimulating. They produce an energetic feeling, caused by the action of caffeine on the brain, which reacts shortly after a person ingests it. Caffeine acts directly on the body by affecting the chemical reactions within the body's cells. It also acts indirectly on the body by increasing the release of hormones, which stimulate cell activity.

Harmful Effects of Caffeine

Large amounts of caffeine can produce insomnia plus increased heart rate and high blood pressure, which can make heart disease worse. Small amounts of caffeine also appear to prevent exhaustion by making more energy available to the muscles. But, as the body relies more heavily on caffeine to feel energetic, headaches and a greater sense of exhaustion are felt when caffeine levels drop.

The drug also increases the production of stomach acid and upsets the action of the intestines, which can lead to the development of stomach and intestinal ulcers (bleeding sores). Because it increases urination, caffeine can cause the body to expel large amounts of necessary minerals. Caffeine has been linked to birth defects, and most doctors advise pregnant women to drink very few or no caffeine beverages during pregnancy.

Other Stimulants

Some drugs that are medically prescribed are occasionally abused by people seeking stimulation. Common among these drugs are diet pills and cold medicines. (Many cold medicines contain caffeine to control the drowsiness often caused by the other ingredients.)

Psychedelics, like stimulants, increase alertness. In fact, alertness is increased to such a large extent that the user often notices every detail of his or her surroundings, creating a kind of hyperstimulation. When a drug user is hyperstimulated, there is frequently too much information being taken into the brain. Because the brain is being overloaded with stimuli, it begins to interpret information differently. This change in the brain often causes the distortion of details, making straight lines seem curved, altering sounds, and changing the appearance of colors.

LSD

LSD is the strongest psychedelic drug. It is made in laboratories by mixing a fungus that grows on rye plants with chemicals. The drug is so strong that a very small amount will produce a powerful effect. In fact, LSD is often soaked into a sugar cube or a small piece of paper, about the size of a postage stamp, which is usually swallowed by the abuser. Some of the slang names for LSD are *acid, blotter, sunshine, blue mist, contact lens, electric Kool-Aid, flash, L, cubes, peace tablets, squirrel, strawberries, owsley, yellows,* and *Zen.*

Effects of LSD on the Brain

LSD speeds up the action in a part of the lower brain that receives signals from the senses. Because LSD alters these signals, it makes smells, sights, sounds, and tastes seem different and often very intense. An object may appear to change its shape and size. A bottle, for example, may seem to melt and become a plate. Walls may seem to move and change color. Senses may be scrambled, a sound may be "seen" as a series of waves, or a color may be sensed as a smell.

LSD users are looking for strange and weird visions of themselves and the world around them. They believe that these experiences can help them to understand themselves better. Many imagine that LSD gives them heightened creativity or improves their talent as an artist, a musician, or an actor.

Effects of LSD on Other Parts of the Body

LSD also affects parts of the body other than the brain. It causes an increase in heart rate, blood pressure, and

A boy experiences the hallucinogenic effects of LSD, a powerful drug that distorts the user's sense of perception and reality. The drug is so strong that very small amounts can cause a person to completely lose control.

body temperature, as well as blurred vision, sweating, chills, headache, dizziness, and vomiting. Effects on the muscles can include severe twitching, weakness, and numbness.

Some people who have taken LSD have what is called a "bad trip." During a bad trip, they have very disturbing visions that are unbearable. In order to escape these visions, they may jump out a window or run out into traffic. Others who are tripping on LSD may think they are superhuman and may shoot or stab themselves.

LSD can reduce certain brain functions and can lead to emotional illness. This can happen to an individual after just one dose of LSD or after regular use of the drug. Included among the emotional problems that can be enhanced by LSD are depression and catatonia. Catatonia is a state characterized by abnormalities of movement and posture. The person's muscles usually become very rigid, causing him or her to remain in the same position for hours without moving.

Unlike cocaine, nicotine, and caffeine, LSD is not addictive. But, whether it is taken only once or many times, it can change the brain forever. Changes in the brain may bring on flashbacks, a repeat of LSD visions— usually repeats of bad trips. Even when a user has not recently taken any LSD, all the effects of a bad trip can return. These flashbacks may come back again and again for years. If the constantly returning visions are very frightening, the person may become emotionally disturbed and may even attempt suicide.

Other Psychedelics

There are other drugs that produce the same kinds of effects as LSD, but LSD's effects are the strongest. Unlike LSD, other psychedelics are made from plants. Mescaline, one such drug, is found in the peyote cactus. Another, psilocybin, comes from mushrooms that grow in Mexico.

Recently, drug dealers have developed psychedelics that are combinations of drugs derived from plants and drugs made in the laboratory. The best known of these human-engineered drugs is STP. STP contains the chemical DOM and the drug atropine. By itself, DOM produces only mild psychedelic effects. When atropine is added to DOM, however, the resulting STP produces psychedelic effects that can last up to five days—and STP's effects on blood pressure and breathing can lead to death. Because of these consequences, abusers often voluntarily stop using STP, which is nonaddictive.

A heroin abuser injects the depressant into a vein in her arm. Most depressants are either injected into the body or taken orally in pill form.

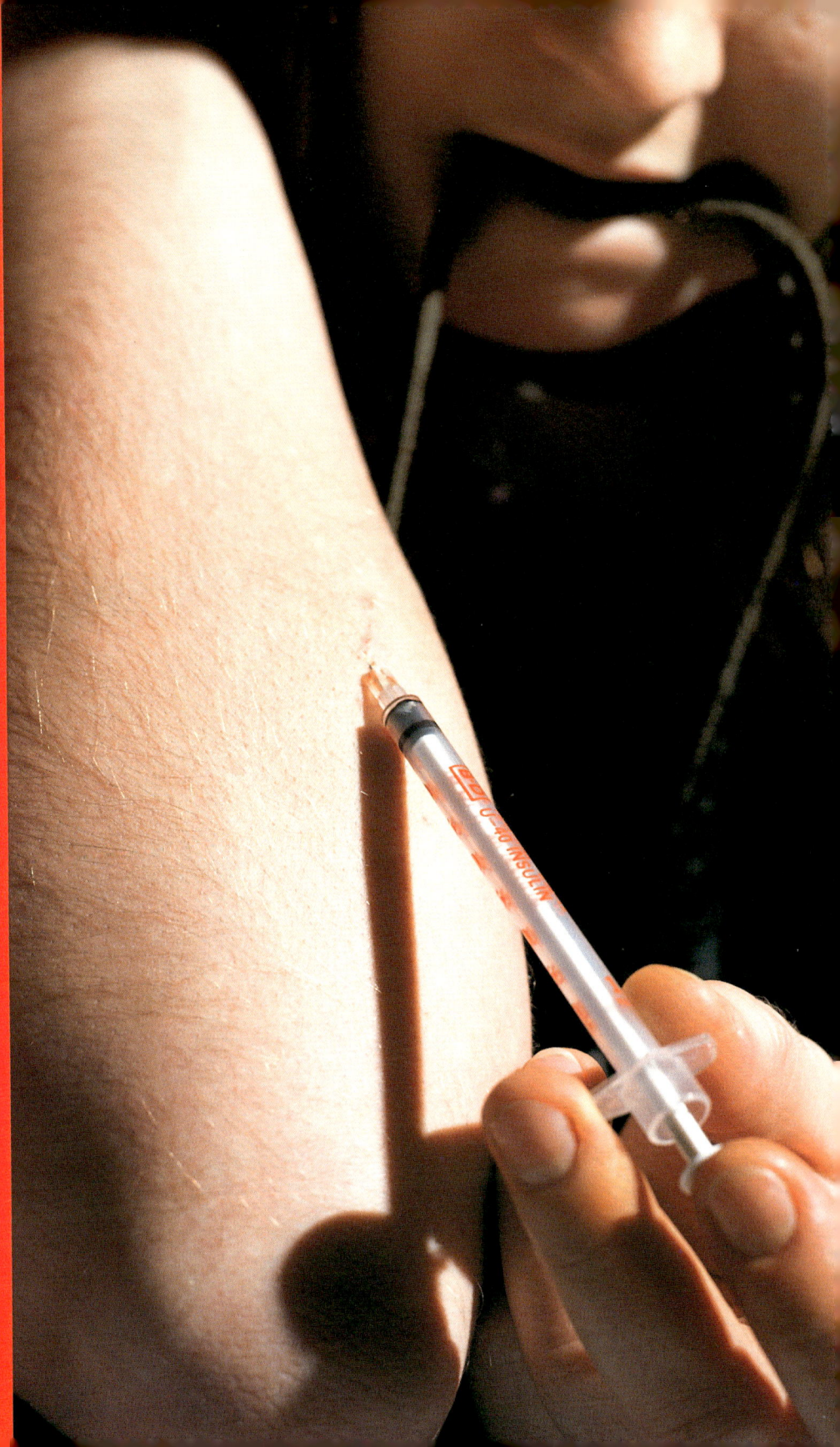

Depressants:
Slowing Down the
Action of the Brain

The first time Tara injected the drug, it made her vomit.
But then she tried it again. This time she took more.
She felt a sudden, pleasant warmth spreading from her
stomach over the rest of her body. She felt protected
and peaceful, as if nothing could harm her. She was so
relaxed that she could hardly speak. Then she became
sleepy and dreamy. Her entire body relaxed, and her
breathing slowed down dramatically. Luckily, her room-
mate noticed that she was breathing strangely. Tara was
rushed to the hospital for treatment. Tara had nearly died.

Tara had taken a depressant—a drug that slows
down, or depresses, the action of the brain. The brain
reduced the signals that it was sending out and, as a
result, Tara's body slowed down. If her body had slowed

down too much, it would have stopped functioning. Minutes later, Tara would have been dead.

Depressants include alcohol, inhalants, and drugs such as barbiturates and narcotics that calm or slow the function of the body. Drugs classified as depressants are manufactured by drug companies and are intended to be used by doctors to treat illnesses of the mind and body. But many people use depressants for nonmedical reasons. Those who abuse depressants are most likely to become physically dependent on them to function. They are also the most likely to overdose or to suffer the various problems that are caused by overuse.

Barbiturates

Barbiturates, the most useful sedatives, were originally developed as medications to treat anxiety and insomnia. Today there are about 50 different kinds of barbiturates.

Uses and Abuses

Doctors use barbiturates to stop pain, to put people to sleep for surgery (anesthesia), to treat convulsions (unconscious state in which a person twitches and jerks), and to treat certain mental illnesses. Like stimulants, barbiturates are addictive and, for this reason, are now seldom used to treat anxiety and insomnia. Other substances—such as tranquilizers—are most often used instead, even though these, too, can be habit-forming.

Barbiturates are the most abused sedatives. They come in small pills or colorful capsules. Some of their slang names are *barbs*, *blues*, *rainbows*, *yellows*, *reds*, *goofballs*, and *phennies*. People who use them are seeking a feeling of drunkenness and peaceful dreaminess, but such drugs have other effects.

The Dangers of Abuse
Barbiturate abusers suffer both physical and mental problems. Breathing, pulse, and heart rate all slow down, and abusers may become dizzy and have trouble speaking clearly. Regular barbiturate use causes many other problems, including emotional instability and general confusion. As a result, users may suddenly laugh, cry, get angry for no reason, or have other drastic mood swings. Users are often unsteady on their feet, making it difficult for them to function effectively.

Barbiturate users find that their bodies build up a tolerance for the drug, so they must take larger and larger amounts to get the effect they seek. This can lead to an overdose, which can cause a person to stop breathing and can cause damage to the heart, nerves, brain, and kidneys. Unless medical care is given at once, a person who has overdosed will die.

Since barbiturates are physically addicting, if an addict suddenly stops taking them, he or she suffers severe withdrawal. Symptoms of withdrawal can include stomach bleeding, cramps, insomnia, and weakness.

Quaaludes
Quaaludes are the most commonly abused sedatives that are not barbiturates. Abusers usually call them *ludes*. Ludes provide a tingling, warm feeling and, in

many people, a desire for sexual relations. Quaalude users feel drawn to total strangers whom they believe are their best friends. As in the case with barbiturates and other addictive drugs, the body eventually becomes tolerant to quaaludes. As this happens, a user takes increasing amounts of the drug to feel any effect. This increased usage can lead to dangerous levels of the drug in the body, which may cause death. Mixing quaaludes with alcohol is a common but extremely dangerous practice. Withdrawal from quaalude addiction is also dangerous and can cause fatal convulsions.

Heroin

Heroin is a narcotic, a powerful depressant that slows down and alters the functions of the body. It is also an opiate, a kind of narcotic made from the opium-poppy plant. Heroin is highly addictive and produces its effect quickly. It is the drug of choice for most narcotic abusers and is the most widely distributed illegal opiate in the world.

Users call heroin by many names: *boys, brown, caballo, chiva, crap, H, hombre, horse, junk, Mexican mud, scag, smack,* and *stuff.* Drug dealers usually mix heroin with other substances such as lactose (milk sugar), a mild laxative, cornstarch, talcum powder, or sometimes other drugs. Because heroin is almost never sold in pure form, users do not really know what they are using. This is a doubly dangerous situation because other substances in heroin can also be highly toxic to the body.

Heroin users usually dissolve the drug in water and inject it into a vein. Sometimes heroin may be drawn into the nose (snorted) or smoked and inhaled.

Those who use heroin are seeking a warm, comfortable feeling with no pain or stress. Like other brain depressors, heroin slows down heartbeat, breathing, and intestinal action. If an abuser overdoses, the body processes slow down so much that he or she may lose consciousness and may die.

The Dangers of Heroin Use

The injection of heroin can cause many problems for users. The use of dirty needles can transmit dangerous diseases such as hepatitis (liver infection). Using dirty needles or previously used needles is also a common way that the deadly AIDS virus is transmitted. Heroin abusers rapidly develop a tolerance for heroin and must therefore constantly take more and more to get any effect. Once an abuser is addicted, his or her body becomes so physically dependent that it is common for all an addict's energies to go into getting more of the drug, causing the addict to cease functioning normally. He or she can't sleep and can't get along with friends or family. The addict forgets to shower or brush his or her teeth. Addicts become angry and sad because increasing amounts of heroin no longer give them the pleasure they remember. Soon, they lose their jobs or drop out of school. Many turn to stealing to get the money they need to buy heroin. Many end up in the hospital, in jail, or dead.

A Painful Withdrawal

If a heroin addict decides to stop taking heroin, he or she will first go through a very difficult period of withdrawal. Then the abuser must fight the hold that heroin has on his or her mind. This process is often slow and painful and may take many years.

The problem of breaking the heroin habit may be related to the effect that heroin has on the brain. Many experts believe that heroin acts like certain body chemicals called endorphins. Endorphins stimulate the brain to produce "good feelings" and a general sense of well-being. When heroin enters the brain, the brain mistakes it for endorphin. As a result, the brain sends a message to the body that no more endorphins are needed, and the body stops making them. The body may not begin to produce endorphins again until long after an addict has stopped using heroin. During that time, the addict craves the good feelings produced only by heroin.

Methadone—taken in liquid or pill form—is a drug that is commonly used to help addicts end their dependence on heroin.

Other Narcotics

Other narcotics, such as morphine, codeine, and Darvon are also occasionally abused by drug addicts. Doctors may prescribe these drugs because they effectively ease pain. Most narcotics are safe in small doses, but sometimes people become so dependent on these drugs to fight their pain that they become addicted. As with other addictive drugs, the more a person relies on a medication to perform functions, the less the body performs. As the body performs less, more and more of a drug is needed to produce the desired effects.

Inhalants

Inhalants are volatile chemicals—those that easily turn into vapor at room temperature. (As water boils, steam is released. The steam is vapor. But the water has to be very hot to make lots of vapor. Volatile chemicals make lots of vapor at room temperature.) Inhalant abusers breathe in these vapors from a rag or plastic bag containing a volatile substance, which is then carried from the lungs to the brain by the blood.

Common Inhalants

The most commonly abused inhalants include solvents (antifreeze, gasoline, nail-polish remover, glue, cleaning fluid, lighter fluid, transmission fluid, paint, varnish, paint thinner) and products in spray cans, such as hair spray, spray paint, and silicone lubricants. Several substances used for medical purposes are also abused. One of these is nitrous oxide, or laughing gas, an anesthetic commonly used by dentists. Another is amyl nitrate, a heart medication, or butyl nitrate, which is a copy of amyl nitrate. These drugs are commonly called *poppers* or *snappers*.

Harmful Effects of Inhalants

Little is known about how inhalants affect the brain. Most are believed to slow brain activity, but some can also stimulate the abuser. In general, inhalants adversely affect the senses of taste, smell, hearing, and touch.

Inhalant abusers are looking for a feeling of great pleasure—a worry-free dreamy feeling, a sense of floating. They may hear and see things that are not there. But after an hour or so, the effects go away. Users then get a head-ache, feel sleepy, and may feel sick to their stomach. Their nose and throat may become irritated.

Certain substances that are commonly inhaled can cause many serious medical problems, such as heart failure and the inability to breathe. Since the dangers are so great, warnings are placed on many inhalants: "Intentional misuse by deliberately concen- trating and inhaling contents can be harmful or fatal." When abused, laughing gas can damage the brain to such a great extent that the user may go into a coma (prolonged unconsciousness) and die.

Vapors from inhalants—such as antifreeze, rubbing alcohol, and gasoline—are breathed in by abusers to produce a dizzy, light-headed feeling.

When used by pregnant women, inhalants can harm the unborn child. Many solvents permanently damage the lungs, liver, kidneys, nerves in the hands and feet, and bone marrow, the material in the center of large bones that makes blood cells.

Alcohol

Alcohol is a chemical made from the sugar of grapes, berries, or molasses, or from the starches of products like corn or rice. These sugars and starches are fermented, or digested, by tiny organisms such as bacteria or yeast. The by-product is alcohol, which is found in beer, wine, and liquor. Drinking these beverages is often a key part of social events such as parties.

People who have one or two drinks over several hours at a party are considered social drinkers. Because the body can break down the alcohol in an average drink in about an hour, drinking at this pace appears to have little effect on people. However, when they drink more rapidly, their bodies can't break down the alcohol fast enough. Soon their thoughts and actions begin to change as the alcohol affects their brain. A person who drinks to this degree on a regular basis is considered an alcoholic. An alcoholic has a dependence on alcohol, usually both mental and physical.

How Alcohol Works

Once it is swallowed, alcohol moves through the stomach and the intestines and passes through the walls of these organs into the blood vessels. The blood then

carries the alcohol through the liver, where some of the alcohol is broken down. Whatever is not broken down moves on to the brain.

Like other brain depressors, alcohol slows down the action of the brain. The more alcohol that is consumed, the more severe the effects. The first section of the brain that is affected is at the top, where speech functions are controlled. Speech often becomes slurred, and the person has trouble thinking. Then the back part of the brain, which controls balance, is affected. A drunk person may stagger or fall while walking. Finally, the inner areas of the brain react to the effects of the alcohol. Emotional control is affected here, and some people become loud and violent. Others may get very quiet and cry. At some point, the brain may slow down so much that the user falls asleep. In some cases, he or she may even lose consciousness. Occasionally, the person's body may be overwhelmed by the slowing effects of the alcohol, and the person may die.

Harmful Effects of Alcohol

Constant exposure to alcohol damages many parts of the body. The stomach and intestines, irritated by alcohol, may develop bleeding ulcers. The liver, which breaks down alcohol, may also become diseased as it becomes overloaded by the constant stress of overuse. One common liver disease of alcoholics, called cirrhosis, damages liver cells. These damaged cells form large swollen areas in the liver. The swollen liver then presses on its major vein, and the pressure can cause internal

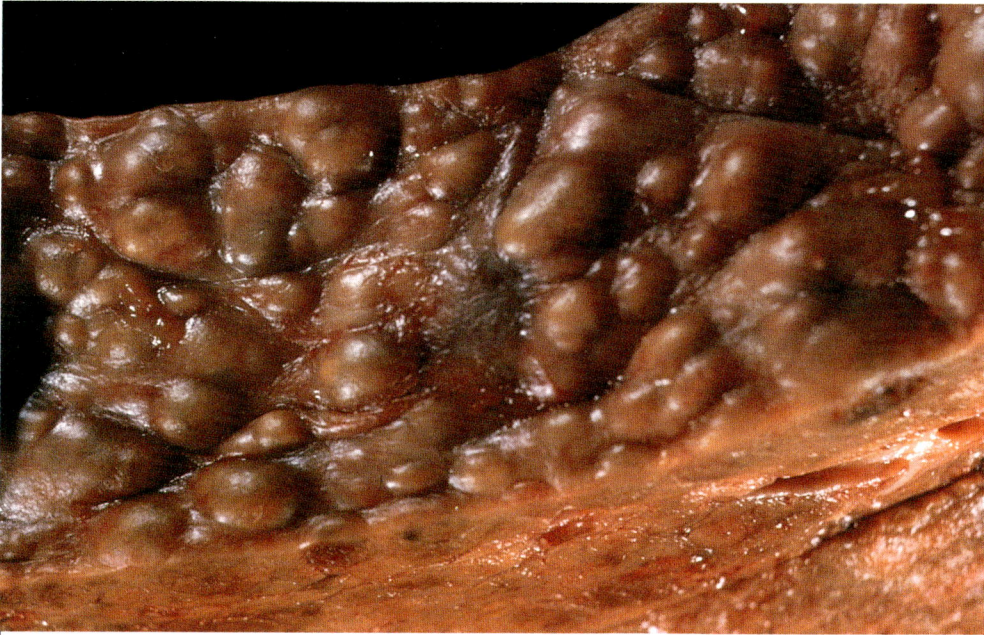

Large, swollen areas can be seen in this photograph of a human liver that is affected by cirrhosis.

bleeding from small veins. Alcohol can also damage the heart, the kidneys, and the brain. Brain damage can cause a person to see or hear things that aren't there and to feel generally anxious and worried.

Alcohol has been linked to a number of different kinds of cancer that affect the mouth, tongue, throat, and esophagus. It can also cause severe damage to a pregnant woman's unborn baby. When a pregnant woman drinks—even two drinks in one day—some of the alcohol passes into the body of her unborn baby. If too much alcohol is passed to the baby, the baby may not develop properly. As a result, it may be deformed in some way, or its internal organs, such as its heart or kidneys, may be abnormal. The baby may have brain damage and lack the ability to learn and to use its arms and legs properly. These problems are commonly called Fetal Alcohol Syndrome (FAS).

Marijuana grows wild in many areas of the world. The leaves of the plant contain THC, which changes perception and sensory intake when it is ingested.

4

PCP and Marijuana: Mixed Effects on the Brain

Ben lit the rolled up leaves and sucked the smoke into his lungs. His heart began to race. A buzzing sound developed in his ears. All kinds of exciting ideas flew through his mind. To him, it seemed as if he were exploring his soul, his innermost thoughts. He felt both happy and a little scared as he began to talk and talk. Everything seemed funny, and he started laughing. The color of the walls began to change. The flowers in the picture on one of the walls seemed to be dancing. Then his excitement changed to calmness. He felt relaxed, and everything seemed comfortable and peaceful.

   Ben had used marijuana, a drug that had mixed effects on his brain. First, his brain was activated—he felt excited and stimulated. Then his brain was depressed— he lost all his energy and felt very tired.

PCP

PCP, another common mixed-effect drug, was originally produced by drug companies. It was designed to put people to sleep before surgery. While it proved to be an excellent anesthetic, PCP also produced very bad side effects. Patients would temporarily "lose their minds," and they would not know where they were. They would see things that weren't there and could become violent. As a result, doctors stopped using PCP during surgery.

PCP is still produced today by drug companies for use as an anesthetic for large animals. But most PCP available from dealers on the street is made in crude kitchen laboratories or in a basement. Many of the people making PCP are not chemists. They sometimes produce substances that are not PCP, but chemicals similar to PCP. There are about 30 such chemicals, each of which produces a variety of different effects—some milder, others stronger than real PCP effects. At least one, called PCC, causes bloody vomiting, diarrhea, and cramps. People who take what they think is PCP cannot be certain of the ingredients or the effects the substance will produce. This problem applies to all street drugs. Drug dealers often substitute PCP for another drug, such as LSD.

PCP, a white powder, may be made into capsules, pills, liquid, or crystals. Sometimes substances are added to the white powder, producing a beige, gray, brown, orange, pink, tan, or yellow powder. Users inhale PCP through their nose, smoke it, swallow it, or inject it into a vein.

PCP has many slang names: *angel dust, Mr. Lovely, supergrass, wacky weed, the pits, tea, rocket fuel, busy bee, Cadillac, crystal, Detroit pink, dummy dust, wolf,* and *zoom.* The names used sometimes indicate the strength of the PCP. Crystal is very strong, dust is often mixed with sugar and is not as strong, rocket fuel is weak, and weed is PCP mixed with marijuana.

How PCP Works

PCP blocks certain signals to the brain and creates a feeling of numbness. People who have taken PCP know they have been touched, but they do not feel anything. Most anesthetics stop all signals from the body's senses—touch, hearing, seeing, smelling, taste—from getting to the brain. PCP, however, blocks only touch (pain) and does not affect a person's breathing and heart rate. This is why it was believed to be an excellent anesthetic.

PCP abusers seek the experience of feeling out of their bodies. They feel stimulated, and their senses are changed so that objects and people around them take on different shapes, colors, and sounds. In the beginning they often feel very happy and at the same time comfortable and relaxed in their surroundings.

Harmful Effects of PCP

PCP abusers can also experience uncomfortable effects. They may find some distortions of their senses frightening, as when a friend appears to be an angry "monster." Users may fear that people are going to hurt them, or they may get frightened and confused because they do not know where they are. This anxiety can sometimes turn into violent behavior.

The effects of PCP may last for as long as six hours. During that time, abusers may have trouble speaking; using their hands, arms, and legs; seeing; and thinking. If they have taken a large dose of PCP, abusers may even become temporarily insane and violent.

PCP also produces some long-term harmful effects, including addiction. Many of the ill effects previously described may not go away for up to a year. Some people feel very sad and try to kill themselves. Others can hurt people around them when they become frightened. Some abusers think they can walk on air and may fall to their deaths as they walk off buildings or cliffs.

Marijuana

Marijuana plants grow as weeds in many parts of the world. The chemical in these plants that acts on the brain is called cannabinoid, or THC. Different kinds of marijuana plants make different amounts of THC. Growing the plant in certain ways can increase the amount of THC that is produced. THC is in all parts of the plant—leaves, stems, flowers, and seeds. The plant also makes a sticky substance called resin, which oozes out of the plant onto the leaves and contains large amounts of THC. There are five kinds of marijuana:

Grass is made up of dried chopped leaves, stems, and seeds. In 100 ounces of grass, there are 1 to 2 ounces of THC.

Sinsemilla is grass made of a plant that has larger amounts of THC than grass. In 100 ounces of sinsemilla there are about 6 ounces of THC.

Hashish is made of dried flowers, leaves, and resin. In 100 ounces of hashish there are 8 to 14 ounces of THC.

Hash oil is the plant's resin. In 100 ounces of hash oil there are 15 to 40 ounces of THC.

Hash-oil crystals are dried resin. In 100 ounces of hash-oil crystals there are about 60 ounces of THC.

These different kinds of marijuana may be mixed together to provide different amounts of THC. Thus the person buying marijuana often has little idea how strong the substance really is.

All kinds of marijuana may be smoked as cigarettes or in a pipe, and sometimes it is added to food. A person eating food that contains marijuana may feel many strange effects. Some of these effects can be extremely uncomfortable and disturbing.

Slang names for marijuana include *roach, pot, m.j., mary jane, dope, grass, reefer, hemp, weed, smoke, herb*, and *hash oil*.

Why People Use Marijuana

People often use marijuana because they like the good feelings it produces. Users think these feelings help to make music, food, and sex better; and they enjoy the way things around them appear changed. Colors, shapes, and sounds seem more intense. Many marijuana users believe the drug makes them more sociable, allowing them to have more fun with others. Some people use marijuana to forget their unhappiness with themselves and life. Sometimes users are angry with their families or friends, and they use marijuana as an act of defiance or to forget their anger.

The effects of marijuana can last up to eight hours. During that time, the user has trouble with motor skills (walking, talking, coordination), remembering, and thinking. The user may also have trouble operating machinery, including driving a car.

Harmful Effects of Marijuana

The regular use of marijuana can harm important parts of the body. Like cigarette smoke, marijuana smoke contains carbon monoxide, which impairs the oxygen-carrying ability of the blood. This means extra stress is placed on the heart because it must work harder to move the blood through the body.

Marijuana smoke also contains higher amounts of tars and irritating chemicals than does cigarette smoke. These tars and chemicals damage the throat, windpipe, and lungs.

Because marijuana increases the heartbeat, heavy use of it may cause added stress to the heart and blood vessels. Marijuana also affects the body's system of fighting infection and its production of hormones, which control important body activities. In addition, marijuana changes the brain's chemistry, causing a disturbance in the way the brain controls the mind and body. With heavy use, memory, thinking, emotional stability, and intelligence may be permanently affected.

For many drug abusers, the first step toward recovery is learning to accept oneself without relying on mind-altering substances.

5

Getting Off Drugs: Healing the Mind and the Body

Paul was a drug abuser. He was 16 years old when he tried to kill himself. He felt intense anger and sadness and didn't want to live anymore.

But Paul turned his life around. He got a lot of help from Dr. Allen L. Carter, who directs the treatment of child and teen drug abusers at the Institute of Living in Hartford, Connecticut. Dr. Carter remembers the day Paul turned up at his office. "His hair was long and dirty. In fact, he was dirty all over. He was wearing earrings, a T-shirt with some kind of death head on it, and jeans decorated with drawings of marijuana leaves. He was angry, and he had a big-time attitude problem."

Dr. Carter found that Paul had used marijuana every day for two and a half years. He had consumed alcohol every other day and had mixed in various drugs along the way. Paul's drug abuse had produced some ugly results. His once-athletic body had become pale and skinny. He had stopped playing basketball and football, and he had dropped out of school and begun running with a new set of drug-using friends.

Drugs had damaged Paul's memory—he couldn't even remember what he had eaten for breakfast two hours earlier. He was angry with himself, his family, and his friends, and he felt worthless. Moreover, Paul was carrying a terrible secret inside himself. A neighbor had sexually abused him when he was 11. Every time Paul thought about what his neighbor had done to him, he felt terrible shame and pain. One of the reasons he took drugs was to make the pain go away.

"About a week after he began treatment, he ran away," says Dr. Carter. "He wanted more drugs. But he came back two days later on his own. He knew he had problems."

Paul was in a program at the Institute of Living for three months. "He believed that the drugs were the answer to his problems with school and family," says Dr. Carter. "Drugs also helped when his friends mistreated him. But gradually with our help, he came to see that it was the other way around. Drugs were causing the problems. Then he was on the way to conquering his drug-abuse problem."

Paul completed the Institute of Living program. Afterward, he joined Narcotics Anonymous, an organization that supports recovering drug abusers as they try to reenter society as productive individuals. He went

back to school, graduated, and joined the army. In a short while, he was accepted into the officer-candidate training program.

"That angry, depressed, unhealthy young man certainly changed for the better," says Dr. Carter. "He, like all drug addicts, had to first admit he had a problem."

According to Dr. Carter, most addicts deny that they have a problem. While others may recognize their problem, addicts usually don't until something shakes them up, like having an auto accident or losing their best friend. Incidents such as these can make addicts realize their drug abuse caused these things to happen. It is then, when they have "hit bottom," as they say, that they decide to reach out to others for help.

Addicts who enter a treatment program learn that they will always be addicted. Drugs have changed their bodies, so they will always react differently to the drug than would normal individuals. Drug addicts must learn to live with addiction.

Detoxification

The first step in almost any drug-treatment program is to "detox." Detox, or detoxification, means to stop using the drug and to get through the accompanying physical pain, known as withdrawal. In most cases this process takes approximately a week, depending on the drug and the amount of abuse. The abused drug is sometimes given in smaller and smaller amounts in order to help the addict's body get used to being without it. At the Institute of Living, medicine is also given to relieve very serious withdrawal effects, such as delirium tremens, which can cause an alcoholic to become very excited and violent. The medicine calms down addicts so they won't hurt themselves or others.

Some of the most difficult withdrawal effects are those produced by heroin withdrawal. These effects resemble a bad case of the flu—sweating, chills, vomiting, muscle cramps and pain, stomach pain, twitching, and sleeplessness. Cocaine withdrawal causes extreme sadness and irritability. The addict's body has come to rely on the pleasurable effect produced by cocaine and reacts badly without it. As mentioned before, cocaine has caused the body to stop making endorphins, the natural chemicals that produce pleasure. It takes a long time for the body to begin making endorphins in normal amounts again.

Dealing with Life's Problems

Once the addict's body is free of the drug, he or she moves on to the next part of the treatment. Dr. Carter explains: "Addicts use drugs to ease the everyday hurts and stresses of life. If someone hurts their feelings or they have an exam, they take drugs. In recovery, they have to learn to cope with the normal problems of life without using drugs."

To begin with, addicts must change the way they live parts of their lives. How do they do that? "They've got to change their social life, the drug-using life. They have to drop friends who use drugs and stop going to places where drugs are being used," says Dr. Carter.

During the time when they are on drugs, addicts often "act out," or become cruel or nasty to their family and their friends. "We urge them to say they're sorry and to try to make up for the unpleasant things," states Dr. Carter.

Addicts may also have many emotional problems that must be solved; the drugs have left them angry and sad. "We help them to develop a new attitude about life—a positive attitude. They need to learn how to be happy, so we talk with them about being grateful for what they have. We suggest that they make a list of the good things about their lives—friends, family, health," says Dr. Carter.

Some addicts have emotional problems that are unrelated to drugs. They use drugs to ease these problems, which are often caused by painful memories, such as past experiences with sexual abuse, as in Paul's case. They may be afraid of certain things, such as getting failing grades, or they could be feeling guilty about something they did. Perhaps they are angry because they feel they are treated unfairly by other people because of race or social status. Addicts often hide all these "true" feelings from others, and they use drugs to help them cover over their true and painful feelings. When they stop taking the drugs, they are simply left with the pain.

"We know that sharing these painful things, talking about them to an understanding person, will help," says Dr. Carter who further explains: "We start by saying, 'Tell me about your life.' Sometimes, as we talk, people

DRUG USE BY U.S. HIGH SCHOOL STUDENTS, 1990

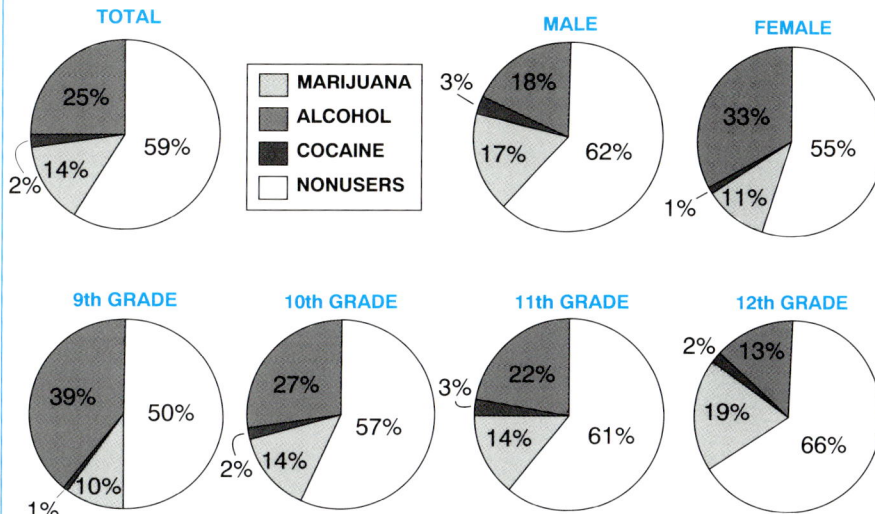

TOTAL

25% · 59% · 14% · 2%

Legend:
- MARIJUANA
- ALCOHOL
- COCAINE
- NONUSERS

MALE

3% · 18% · 17% · 62%

FEMALE

33% · 55% · 1% · 11%

9th GRADE

39% · 50% · 10% · 1% · 2%

10th GRADE

27% · 57% · 14% · 2%

11th GRADE

3% · 22% · 14% · 61%

12th GRADE

2% · 13% · 19% · 66%

Source: U.S. Department of Health and Human Services, Centers for Disease Control, *Morbidity and Mortality Weekly Report* (November 15, 1991).

burst out with all kinds of things—things they have never shared before. We talk about these situations, and we try to figure out why it hurts to remember them. Just talking about the pain helps to ease it.

"Another problem addicts must face once they have stopped using drugs is social isolation. They have lived a life where drugs were really all they needed for company. They are not sure how to get along with other people, and they often feel inferior to other people. They feel very alone and bad about using drugs.

"What they need is to share their feelings with other addicts. When they do, they learn that others have the same troubles and fears they do. They feel less alone, part of a group. This is what a group session does."

In a group session, six or eight addicts meet with a counselor. They talk about the difficulties of getting off drugs and give one another advice. Comments such as "that happened to me" or "I did that stuff, too," help the addicts feel support. With the counselor's help, they also make sure that everyone in the group faces problems honestly. For example, someone may describe an argument with a brother. "He doesn't understand. He doesn't know how hard it is to get off drugs." The counselor may ask the others to suggest reasons the argument may not be the brother's fault.

Dr. Carter describes the treatment goal: "Through all of these methods we are trying to help the addict get rid of the anger and sadness. Being angry and sad is just one step from going back to drugs. Our goal is to teach them to be happy. If they can learn to be happy and grateful to be alive, they'll never go back to drugs."

After Treatment

About 80 percent of addicts who enter the Institute of Living program successfully complete it. Some people may have to go through a drug-abuse program five or six times before they manage to get permanently free of drug abuse. Once a person has completed the Institute of Living program, he or she is urged to join Alcoholics Anonymous or Narcotics Anonymous. These organizations have programs that help addicts keep the positive feelings they need to stay off drugs.

Treatment programs can help the addict learn how to live without drugs. But the addict may often be left

ALCOHOL USE IN THE UNITED STATES, BY AGE AND SEX, 1988

	TOTAL	
	18–29	7,818,000
	30–44	5,096,000
	45–64	1,989,000
	65+	392,000
	MALE	
	18–29	5,394,000
	30–44	3,931,000
	45–64	1,577,000
	65+	330,000
	FEMALE	
	18–29	2,424,000
	30–44	1,165,000
	45–64	412,000
	65+	62,000

Source: U.S. Department of Health and Human Services, National Institute on Alcohol Abuse and Alcoholism.

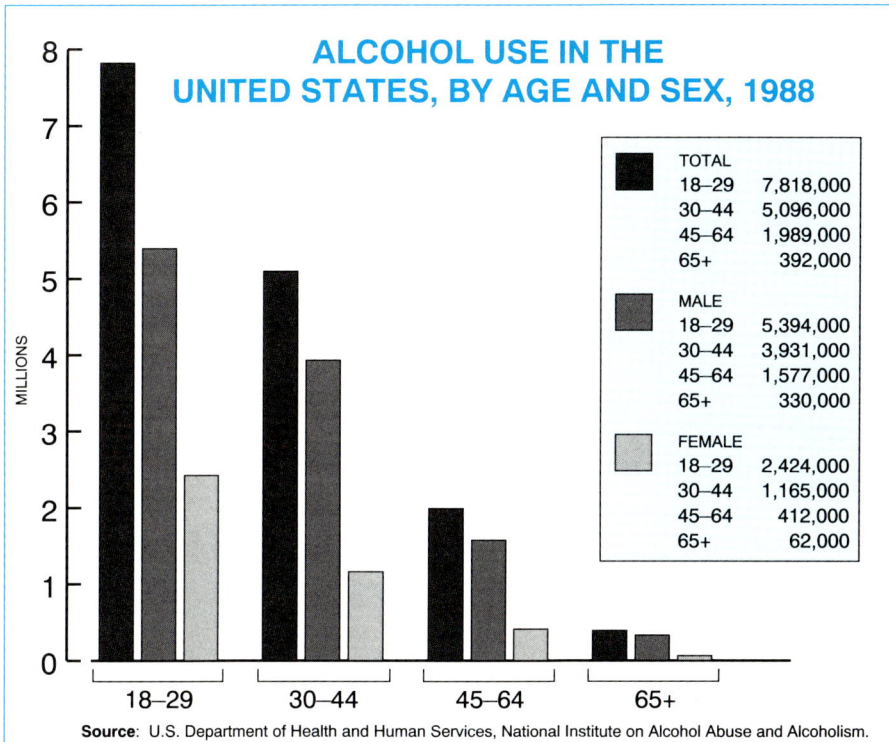

with problems caused by drugs that cannot be cured. Damage to the brain may affect memory, thought, and intelligence. Drugs may damage such important parts of the body as the heart, the kidneys, and the liver.

Dr. Carter has some advice for those young people who are using or considering using drugs. "You need to understand that drugs are powerful and dangerous. Everyone believes they are stronger than the power of drugs. They believe they can 'handle it.' But the sad fact is that few people can resist dependency on addictive drugs. Down through history, drugs have destroyed millions and millions of people. Don't forget that alcohol is a drug. It is the deadliest chemical that teenagers use. It is the number one killer of those 15 to 24 years

Alcohol abuse is one of the major causes of fatal car accidents in America. The National Health Survey estimates that more than 15 million Americans have some form of alcohol dependence.

old. Alcohol causes many fatal auto accidents, other accidents, and suicide among this age group. About 10,000 young people in the USA will die this year because of using alcohol."

Thanks to programs such as Dr. Allen L. Carter's at the Institute of Living and all the other programs throughout the country, many teenagers will be able to conquer their drug dependencies and look forward to happy and productive lives.

Glossary

alcoholic A person who drinks excessive amounts of alcohol, becoming dependent on it.

anesthesia The loss of all sensation, produced by a drug to stop pain during surgery.

bad trip Bad effects, usually frightening visions, that are produced by drug abuse.

brain activator A drug that speeds up the brain's activity.

brain depressor A drug that slows down the brain's activity.

carbon monoxide A gas that is produced by burning. It can cause oxygen starvation for the smoker.

convulsion A spasm that causes a person to lose consciousness, twitch, and jerk.

detoxification The process of stopping the use of a drug and going through the pain of withdrawal from it.

drug A chemical that changes the way the body functions.

drug abuser A person who uses a drug for the pleasure that it produces.

drug addict A drug abuser who has become dependent on the effects of a drug.

drug tolerance The body's resistance to a drug's effects.

endorphin A chemical made by the body that triggers the areas of the brain that cause people to feel pleasure.

flashback A frightening vision that returns many times, long after the abuser has taken the drug that caused it.

hallucinate To sense something that isn't there.

inhalant A solvent or other volatile chemical whose vapors are breathed in by an abuser.

narcotic A drug made from the opium poppy or manufactured by a drug company for use as a painkiller.

overdose An excessive amount of a drug that causes severe illness and sometimes death.

physical dependence The development of the body's need for a drug to help it function.

psychedelic A drug that causes a person to see things that aren't there.

psychoactive drug A drug that acts on the brain.

psychological dependence The mental craving for a drug.

sedative A drug such as a sleeping pill that calms a person.

stimulant A drug that makes a person feel alert and energetic.

stroke Damage to the brain caused by the rupture or blockage of a blood vessel supplying the brain.

tar A chemical substance that is produced by the burning of a cigarette. Tar can damage the lungs of a smoker.

withdrawal The physical discomfort and mental pain that occur when an addicted person stops using a drug.

Further Reading

Berger, Gilda, and Berger, Melvin. *Drug Abuse A–Z.*
Hillside, NJ: Enslow, 1990.
Chomet, Julian. *Speed & Amphetamines.* New York:
Franklin Watts, 1990.
Condon, Judith. *Pressure to Take Drugs.* New York:
Franklin Watts, 1990.
Hawley, Richard. *Drugs & Society.* New York: Walker,
1992.
Turck, Mary C. *Crack & Cocaine.* New York: Crestwood
House, 1990.
Yoslow, Mark. *Drugs in the Body: Effects of Abuse.* New
York: Franklin Watts, 1992.

Where to Find Help

Alanon Family Groups
P.O. Box 862
Midtown Station
New York, NY 10018

Alcohol and Drug Services
 Administration
1300 1st Street, N.E.
Washington, D.C. 20002

Alcoholics Anonymous World
 Services
Box 459
Grand Central Station
New York, NY 10163

American Cancer Society
P.O. Box 190429
Atlanta, GA 31119

American Heart Association
7272 Greenville Avenue
Dallas, TX 75231

American Lung Association
1740 Broadway
New York, NY 10019

Cocaine Abuse Hot Line
1-800-568-3303

National Clearinghouse for Alcohol
 and Drug Information
P.O. Box 2345
Rockville, MD 20852

National Institute on Drug Abuse
1-800-662-HELP

Index